PIERO DELLA FRANCESCA

The World's Masters – *New Series*

by Anthony Bertram

THE STUDIO PUBLICATIONS, LONDON & NEW YORK

FIRST PUBLISHED 1949

WORLD'S MASTERS NEW SERIES *Editor: ANTHONY BERTRAM*

The covers of this series, designed by Arthur Hundleby, are based on heraldic motives representing the national school to which each artist belongs or with which he is chiefly associated

Already published

WILLIAM BLAKE

SANDRO BOTTICELLI

JAN VERMEER OF DELFT

HANS HOLBEIN THE YOUNGER

WILLIAM HOGARTH

JEAN AUGUSTE DOMINIQUE INGRES

PIETER BRUEGEL

EL GRECO

MICHELANGELO

In preparation

MATHIAS GRÜNEWALD

EUGENE DELACROIX

JEROME BOSCH

THE VAN EYCKS

REMBRANDT VAN RIJN

Printed in Great Britain by William Clowes & Sons Ltd, London and Beccles. Published in London by The Studio Ltd, 66 Chandos Place, WC2, and in New York by the Studio Publications Inc, 381 Fourth Avenue

Introduction

PIERO DELLA FRANCESCA wrote and painted; but he did not express himself artistically in two mediums, like Blake or Michelangelo; nor did he write memoirs or art criticism like Messrs. X and Y. He wrote the *Prospettiva Pingendi*, a technical treatise in which 'he carried on the science of perspective to the point at which it remained for several centuries' (Waters); and, in his old age, 'that his mind might not vegetate—*ne ingenium inertia torpesceret*', as he said, the *Libellus de Quinque Corporibus Regularibus*, in which he applied Euclid to art. The five regular bodies involved were the triangle, cube, octahedron, dodecahedron and icosahedron.

I fancy that those who believe in the 'inspiration' of art and the 'fine frenzy' as something utterly foreign, even opposed, to the rational and objective processes of mathematical thought, may find the icosahedron, as Bridges found Hopkins's longest poem, 'a great dragon folded in the gate to forbid all entrance'. They hate every one of its twenty plane faces.

But before asserting that the icosahedron has nothing to do with art, they should modestly remind themselves that Piero believed it had; and that Plato affirmed that 'circles and globes, and such rectangles as are made by rules and squares . . . are beautiful at all times by themselves and in their very nature'.

Indeed, the artists of the Renaissance found no opposition between art and any branch of science. On the contrary, they

3

believed that each might serve the other; that knowledge and vision, intellect and intuition could be integrated in the one complete man. We may take Leonardo da Vinci as the most obvious demonstration of this; but also, perhaps, as the last. After him, the high road of our civilization bifurcated: art and science took their different and diverging ways. Perhaps that was the chief cause of its disintegration.

We shall get nowhere with Piero if we take the 'isolationist' view of art. It is by a geometric beauty—austere, rarefied, impersonal, intellectual—that he commands our attention. . . .

But that is quite the wrong phrase. He *commands* us nothing: he is not sufficiently interested in us. He builds his crystal world and leaves the door open: we may go in, if we choose; but Piero is no longer there. With unhurried majesty, he has withdrawn—always—before our clumsy intrusion. That, I suppose, is what Berenson felt when he wrote that 'impersonality . . . is his most distinguishing virtue'. What Piero has created *is*: you may take it or leave it; he will neither command, nor charm, nor advertise. *He is not there.*

But, of course, he has been there, a living, passionate artist. He has left a brightness behind, an emotion *after* it has been recollected in tranquillity. There is, I feel, much affinity between him and Wordsworth; but his work is one stage further removed from his first experience than is the poet's. He poured his white-hot vision into the mould of geometry and left it to set quite cold before turning it out. Any other means he at times employed to express that vision, whether tenderness or drama, psychology, movement or rhythm of light and shade—I shall touch on some of these later —are always subordinate to this means of logical construction. His picture can stand up four-square; and that is as essential to its

4

whole existence as if it were indeed a building.

It is conspicuous, and not surprising, how large a part the representation of architecture plays *in* his pictures, and how profoundly he understands it. But that, of course, is not what I am talking about. I am talking about the architecture *of* his pictures, in which the trees or the human beings are as much part as are column or entablature. In fact, it is the first duty of his human beings to be sound structural members.

There is no more striking example of this than *The Flagellation* (Plate xi). All ugliness and dramatic violence, all tragedy and pain are expelled. We are introduced, instead, into a serene and stately world, where the figures are but units in a monumental demonstration of order.

Let us look a little more closely at two other examples. First, *The Resurrection* (Plate xxxiii). It is instructive to compare this with such a very opposite treatment as El Greco's in the Prado picture (Plate x in the *Greco* of this series), where the construction is based on an isosceles triangle balanced on a very acute point—a most uneasy, baroque triangle. But Piero's is an equilateral triangle standing firmly on its base and often repeated, with variations. The base of the dominant vertical triangle coincides with that of the picture; its apex is at Christ's chin. A secondary vertical triangle has its base along the top of the tomb, its apex at the top of Christ's head. A third has its base along the tomb, but it stops at the right of the soldier's neck (the soldier with the lance); its apex is the point of the flag-staff. Outside them all is the suggestion of a greater, mostly invisible triangle. We see the fragments of its sides against the sky, up the tops of the trees on the right and the dome-shaped hill on the left; and we discover that they would meet on a continuation of the flag-staff. The triangle is repeated in little again and again; for example, in the crooked legs of the front soldiers; inverted between them; joining the points of their knees to the head of the far soldier; from Christ's left hand to where the top of the tomb is cut by the two necks; and so on and so on. All this, however, is only façade—a construction in two dimensions. But if we look a little closer we see that this triangle appears also horizontally, its base along the front edge of the picture, its apex at Christ's invisible foot. And again we find it, beyond, splaying out from that foot along the lines of the trees to an unstated base across the hills. Again, we find it constantly in little, sometimes most subtly suggested. For example, the crooked leg of the left soldier, which gave us a vertical triangle, shares its undrawn base with a horizontal triangle whose apex is the invisible right hand of the soldier beyond.

This is the merest beginning of an analysis. It omits, for example, all reference to the intricate series of curves which plays over these variations on a triangle, as a similar series plays, in my second example, *The Nativity* (Plate xliv), over variations on a rectangular lattice. It is particularly fascinating to follow the horizontal of that lattice through its variations. At the top of the penthouse roof it is stated clearly. It descends to the eave with only two major interruptions: the tuft on the right, which corresponds with one of the major verticals, that passing through the Virgin and the shepherd's raised arm; and the bird, which corresponds to the other major vertical, that passing through the shadow, the dark angel and the Infant's head. The horizontal then breaks into choppy waves along the angels' and shepherds' heads, and into a most complicated variation along the guitars and the heads of the Virgin and St Joseph. It is restated more quietly along the bottom of the angels' dresses, where, after a break, it is picked up by the top of the saddle.

6

It fades out in the lower part of the picture into what might be described as a horizontal feeling, in which the Infant plays His conspicuous part. I must leave the reader to discover other members of this construction, but I cannot omit indicating the great triangle which sweeps away from the Infant into the far landscape on the left and to Borgo San Sepolcro on the right.

I must also leave the reader to search out elsewhere Piero's architectural characteristics—the noble balance of the rectilinear figures, the slow swing of the curves like those of domes and crescents, the steady beat of the perspective.

We have seen, then, how the impersonality of Piero's beings is conveyed by their subordination to a greater, an embracing structural entity, as dancers are to the whole ballet. But it is also conveyed psychologically. They look straight before them with ecstatic eyes, neither at us nor at one another. Could anything be less like a 'conversation piece' than those three figures on the right of *The Flagellation* (Plate xi)? Each is alone; and each gazes rapt on the unseen, like the companions of the Queen of Sheba (Plate xx), pensive and enigmatic, and but half of this world.

Our Lady of Mercy (Plate iii) extends her protection in serene universality, without any self-indulgence in compassion or indeed any personal engagement. Hers is a catholic and eternal mercy that is not stirred by particular instance. She is big with mercy, as in *The Madonna del Parto* (Plate xiii) she is big with the Godhead.

But Piero is not a mystic painter. His Christ (Plates i and xxxiii) is the perfect man, robust, athletic. The bodies he paints are solid, massive, articulated, standing firmly on the ground. It is this which most markedly differentiates him from the purely religious painters —the Sienese of the early fourteenth century, for example, whose beings are altogether not of this world. Piero, like Blake, saw a

7

double vision—the God *and* the Man, the God in man, but the man also in Man. Therefore he can also show the human drama of Adam (Plate xvii), who sees death with tense expectancy, or of Eve, who is absorbed in her vision of loss and inevitability—Eve, who brought death into the world and sees it reaping its first harvest. But as, beside this motionless inward drama, we may see the externalized grief of the lamenting man (Plate xvi), so also in *The Crucifixion* (Plate vii) we may see Piero using both his methods of drama and impersonality in the same work. We contemplate quite a different Madonna from those we have hitherto remarked. The detachment of her sovereignty is gone, and Piero charges her with tragic emotion to express a particular mother's pain, as he charges St John (Plate ix), through his immense gesture, with a companion ecstasy of private grief. Here it is Christ that hangs impersonal and imperturbable. Christ, who is the most engaged, laying down His life, achieves the highest detachment. At the summit of suffering, the majestic spirit finds peace.

But even when externalized, Piero's drama usually lacks conflict: it is like that of the *St. Michael* (Plate xlv). His power and his battle are expressed in his confident supremacy. Piero can afford to reduce the dragon to almost ridiculous proportions without lowering the value of the archangel's victory.

But there *are* conflicts in Piero (Plate xxix). In their movement and realism he displays himself as a man of the Renaissance, a discoverer. I could have dealt only with that aspect of him and filled my little space to overflowing. It could be shown how he developed the full modelling of his figures and their psychological and dramatic realism from Masaccio and Donatello, and his perspective from Uccello; and how he handed on these qualities to his pupils, Signorelli and Melozzo da Forli; and how, in *The Dream*

8

of Constantine (Plate xxiv), he made astounding researches in chiaroscuro, which were to serve Rembrandt and Leonardo da Vinci after him; and how in portraiture (Plate xl) he could descend from his lofty contemplation of external relationships to a close study and subtle revelation of individual character. In short, Piero could be 'placed' in the history of art as one whose discoveries were among the most important in the movement towards materialism. But however much his science and his skill belong to the beginning of an age that was to achieve our present chaos, his spirit was mediaeval. The world of his vision was inhabited by great hierarchs celebrating the ritual of being. He interrupts and fixes its image in unalterable order, balance and proportion. He imposes an eternal stillness on the measured movement and an eternal silence on the chant. But the distillation of all power and music is enclosed in the stillness and silence of his living geometry.

> Words move, music moves
> Only in time; but that which is only living
> Can only die. Words, after speech, reach
> Into the silence. Only by the form, the pattern
> Can words or music reach
> The stillness, as a Chinese jar still
> Moves perpetually in its stillness.

References.—The references to Waters and Berenson are from books listed in the Bibliographical Notes. Plato is quoted from the *Philebus* xxxi, in F. A. Paley's translation, and Bridges from his edition of Gerard Manley Hopkins. The closing passage is from T. S. Eliot's *Burnt Norton.*

Biographical Notes

Between 1410–1420.   Piero di Benedetto dei Franceschi, called della Francesca, born at Borgo San Sepolcro, in the valley of the upper Tiber. His father was a shoemaker of an established and respectable family. No precise date of birth has been determined.

1439.   In Florence, working with Domenico Veniziano. All trace of their collaboration is lost.

1445.   Commissioned to paint an altarpiece (Plates II–X) by the Confraternity of the Misericordia at Borgo.

1446–1447?   Apparently in Loreto with Veniziano, but again all trace of work is lost.

1451.   At Rimini, working for Sigismondo Malatesta. Possibly also in Ferrara.

c. 1452.   Probably in Rome. Our information is confused and unreliable on all his movements about this time. He wandered extensively in central and north Italy.

After 1452.   Took over decoration of Bacci chapel in San Francesco, Arezzo, which Bicci di Lorenzo had been commissioned to execute in 1446. The latter died in 1452. Work was completed before 1566.

1469.   In Umbria, as guest of Raphael's father, Giovanni Santi. Subsequent activities are but vaguely recorded. He was definitely in Borgo in 1478 and made his will in 1487.

1492.   12 October. Died and was buried in the Badia, now the cathedral, at Borgo.

Notes to the Illustrations

The problems of attribution and dating, in the case of many so-called Pieros, are extremely difficult. I have thought it best, with very few exceptions, to follow one authority, Signor Roberto Longhi in his 1942 revised edition (see Bibliographical Notes). Most of his dates are given tentatively and must not be regarded as having more than the value of high probability.

Plate I.
Originally an altarpiece in the Priory of St John the Baptist, Borgo San Sepolcro.

Plate II.
Commissioned on 11 January, 1445, by the Confraternity of the Misericordia, Borgo San Sepolcro, to be delivered by the end of 1448, but the style suggests that it was not finished by that date. The altarpiece has outer wings and a predella by another painter, probably Florentine. They are not reproduced.

Plate X.
The history of this picture is unknown before 1850, when it was acquired by the Accademia at Venice. It is inscribed HIER. AMADI. AVG.F. This has not been satisfactorily explained, and even its authenticity is doubted. Amadi has not been identified.

Plate XI.
The three mysterious figures on the right have not been absolutely identified. The most probable explanation is that the central figure is Od'Antonio da Montefeltro with the two 'evil' counsellors, Manfredo dei Pio and Tommaso dell'Agnello, who were sent to compass his ruin by Malatesta of Rimini (Plate XII). All were assassinated in a popular revolt in 1444. If this is a valid explanation the picture may be of early date, but not necessarily. Other authorities date it as early as 1445 and as late as 1469 Signed: OPUS PETRI DE BURGO SCI SEPULCRI.

Plate XII.

Malatesta commissioned the fresco for the walls of the Chapel of Relics in the Temple of Malatesta, Rimini. It was much over-painted but has recently been restored. It is signed and dated: PETRI DE BURGO OPUS MCCCCLI.

Plate XIII.

Identified as a work of Piero's in 1899. Monterchi is a small village near Borgo San Sepolcro. It is popularly called 'del Parto' because of the obviously pregnant state of the Blessed Virgin.

Plates XV–XXXII.

The great series of frescoes decorating the choir of the church of St Francis in Arezzo was begun by Bicci di Lorenzo, who died in 1452, when Piero took over.

Plates XV and XVII show Adam, who feels the approach of death and asks Seth to seek the Oil of Salvation, which had been promised him, from the angel who guarded the gates of Eden. On the extreme left of Plate XV, Seth is talking with the angel, who, instead of the oil, gives him three seeds to place under Adam's tongue. From these seeds will grow the tree in which man will find his salvation. He returns to find him already dead, and carries out the angel's command, surrounded by the lamenting descendants of Adam (Plate XVI and in middle of Plate XV). The tree is, of course, a symbol of the whole legend.

The seeds grew into a tree, which Solomon felled for use in the construction of the Temple but which the workmen found unsuitable and threw aside. It was laid as a footbridge across the stream of Siloe. The Queen of Sheba, travelling to Jerusalem, arrived at this bridge, and, its future being revealed to her, knelt in adoration (left of Plate XIX). She tells Solomon that when a certain man is crucified on that wood the fall of Israel will be approaching (right of Plate XIX), whereupon Solomon ordered the wood to be buried. The Pool of Bethesda sprang up over the spot, and shortly before the Crucifixion the wood floated to the surface. Plate XXI depicts the wood being carried to its burial (or perhaps for the making of the bridge) with an obvious symbolic reference to Christ's later carrying of the Cross.

It is most puzzling that Piero does not then insert the Crucifixion but the Annunciation (Plate XXII). Perhaps he felt that this beginning of the story

12

of Christ would be adequate to convey His whole history, as he then jumps to the dream which the Emperor Constantine had on the eve of giving battle to the invading Maxentius (Plate XXIV). Constantine saw an angel—in the left top corner, very much damaged—who pointed to a shining cross by his bedside. The work is a remarkable early example of the use of chiaroscuro, the source of light being the angel. In Plate XXV we see Constantine riding out to meet Maxentius, holding out the cross, at the sight of which Maxentius and his troops flee without fighting (this part is almost totally destroyed and we reproduce only the Emperor and his retinue).

The Empress Helena, having in her turn dreamed, searches for the true Cross. In the course of her efforts she orders the torture of a Jew who was supposed to know traditionally where it was hidden. We have not reproduced this scene, which is partly the work of a collaborator, whom Longhi identifies as possibly Giovanni di Piemonte. The Jew having revealed the place, the Empress is present at the exhumation (left of Plate XXVI). Three crosses were found. Christ's Cross raises a dead youth to life and is thus identified (right of Plate XXVI and Plate XXVIII).

Three centuries later Chosroes, King of Persia, seized the Cross and set it up by his own throne. The Emperor Heraclius went out to recover it, which he did successfully in battle (Plate XXIX). We see the battle, and on the right the execution of Chosroes with the Cross by his throne above. In Plate XXXI Heraclius brings the Cross back to Jerusalem. Another hand has also worked on this fresco.

Plate XLI.

Victory stands behind Federigo. Before him are Force, with a broken column; Prudence, with a mirror and double head like Janus, contemplating the past and the future; and Justice, with scales and two-edged sword. Cupid drives.

Plate XLII.

The unicorns symbolize purity. Probably one of the figures behind the Duchess is Truth. Before her sit Faith, with a cross and chalice; and Religion, on whose knee the pelican feeds her young. Cupid drives. The interpretation of these allegories is tentative.

Plate XLV.

St Michael's girdle is inscribed ANGELUS POTENTIA DEI LUCHA, which has led some critics to suppose that Luca Signorelli assisted in the painting. A St Andrew in the Frick Collection, New York, may also have belonged to this altarpiece.

Plate XLVIII.

The hands of Federigo are by another painter, whom Longhi identifies as a Fleming whose work at Urbino is to be recognized in several other paintings. He has established that he was not, as previously thought, Justus of Ghent.

Bibliographical Notes

Longhi, Roberto. *Piero della Francesca*. Milan. Revised and enlarged ed. 1942. This is a standard and invaluable book in Italian. It contains ten pages of Bibliography to which the serious student is referred. All works are illustrated.

Waters, W. G. *Piero della Francesca*. London, 1901. The only book in English known to me. It is not of very great critical or scholarly value, and cannot be relied on for its attributions.

Venturi, A. This eminent critic has written several works on or referring to Piero. The most generally useful is a volume in the series *I grandi maestri dell'arte italiana*. Florence, 1922.

Many other works in Italian and German will be found in Longhi's bibliography. It seems more useful here to draw attention to general works in English where his place in the history of Italian art can be *shortly* studied.

Berenson, B. *Central Italian Painters*. London, 1897 (and later eds.).

Venturi, A. *A Short History of Italian Art*. English ed. 1926.

Holmes, Sir C. *An Introduction to Italian Painting*. London, 1929.

Mather, F. J. *A History of Italian Painting*. New York, 1923.

I. (*Opposite*) BAPTISM OF CHRIST. C. 1440–1445.
Tempera on wood. 166×115 cm. London,
National Gallery.

II. POLYPTYCH OF OUR LADY OF MERCY.
Probably after 1448. Borgo san Sepolcro, Palazzo
Communale. (Photo: Anderson.)

III. OUR LADY OF MERCY. From Plate II. (Photo: Anderson.)

IV. HEAD OF OUR LADY OF MERCY. Detail from opposite plate.
(Photo: Anderson.)

V. ST BENEDICT. From Plate II.

VI. ST BERNADINE. From
Plate II.

VII. (*Opposite*) CRUCIFIXION. From
Plate II.

VIII. HEAD OF CHRIST ON THE
CROSS. Detail from opposite plate.

IX. ST JOHN AT THE FOOT
OF THE CROSS. Detail from
Plate VII.

X. (*Opposite*) ST JEROME
WITH (?) GEROLAMO AMADI
Early work. Tempera on
wood. 47×39 cm. Venice
Accademia. (Plate : Anderson.

XI. THE FLAGELLATION OF CHRIST. ? c. 1460. Tempera on wood. 59 × 81·5 cm. Urbino,
Galleria Nazionale della Marche.

XII. (*Below*) ST SIGISMUND AND PANDOLFO MALATESTA. Dated 1451. Fresco.
Rimini, Temple of Malatesta. (Photo: Anderson.)

XIII. MADONNA AND TWO ANGELS. (Called *The Madonna del Parto*.) ? 1550–
1555. Fresco. Monterchi, Cemetery Chapel. (Photo: Anderson.)

XIV. HEAD OF MADONNA. Detail from opposite plate. (Photo: Anderson.)

XV. THE DEATH OF ADAM. From *The Legend of the Cross*.
(See Notes to the Illustrations.) c. 1551. Fresco. Arezzo,
San Francesco. (Photo: Anderson.)

XVI. (*Opposite*) FIGURES AT THE FEET OF THE DEAD
ADAM. Detail from Plate XV. (Photo: Anderson.)

XVII. THE DYING ADAM WITH EVE, SETH
AND OTHERS. Detail from Plate XV.

XVIII. (*Opposite*) HEAD OF EVE. Detail from
Plate XVII. (Photo : Anderson.)

XIX. THE VISIT OF THE QUEEN OF SHEBA TO SOLOMON.
From *The Legend of the Cross.* c. 1551. Fresco. Arezzo, San Francesco. (Photo : Anderson.)

XX. (*Opposite*) COMPANIONS OF THE QUEEN OF SHEBA.
Detail from Plate XIX. (Photo : Anderson.)

XXI. THE CARRYING OF THE WOOD OF THE CROSS. From *The Legend of the Cross*. c. 1551. Fresco. Arezzo, San Francesco.

XXII (*Opposite*) THE ANNUNCIATION. From *The Legend of the Cross*. c. 1551. Fresco. Arezzo, San Francesco. (Photo: Anderson.)

XXIII. HEAD OF THE MADONNA. Detail from Plate XXII. (Photo: Anderson.)

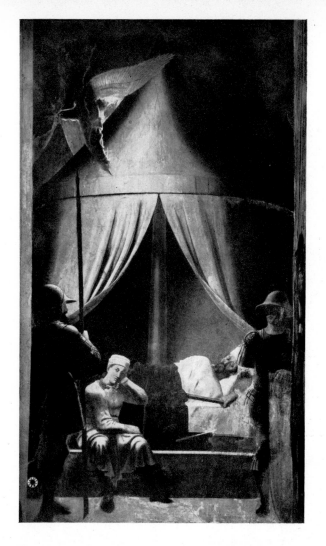

XXIV. THE DREAM OF THE EMPEROR CONSTANTINE. From *The
Legend of the Cross*. c. 1551. Fresco. Arezzo, San Francesco. (Photo: Anderson.)

XXV. DETAIL FROM CONSTANTINE'S VICTORY OVER MAXENTIUS. From *The Legend of the Cross*. c. 1551. Fresco. Arezzo, San Francesco. The remainder of the fresco is very badly damaged. (Photo: Anderson.)

XXVI. DISCOVERY AND TESTING OF THE CROSS. From *The Legend of the Cross*. c. 1551. Fresco. Arezzo, San Francesco. (Photo: Anderson.)

XXVII. Detail from Plate XXVI.

XXVIII. (*Opposite*) THE TESTING OF THE CROSS.
Detail from Plate XXVI.

XXIX. THE VICTORY OF HERACLIUS OVER CHOSROES, KING OF PERSIA. From *The Legend of the Cross.* c. 1551. Fresco. Arezzo, San Francesco. (Photo: Alinari.)

XXX. HEAD OF A TRUMPETER. Detail from opposite plate. (Photo: Alinari.)

XXXI. HERACLIUS RETURNS THE CROSS TO
JERUSALEM. From *The Legend of the Cross*. c. 1551.
Fresco. Arezzo, San Francesco. (Photo: Anderson.)

XXXII. THE FOLLOWERS OF HERACLIUS.
Detail from opposite plate.

XXXIII. THE RESURRECTION. C. 1551. Fresco. Borgo San Sepolcro,
Palazzo Communale. (Photo: Alinari.)

XXXIV. HEAD OF CHRIST. Detail from opposite plate. (Photo: Anderson.)

XXXV. (*Opposite*) ST MARY MAGDALEN.
c. 1551. Fresco. Arezzo, Cathedral. (Photo:
Anderson.)

XXXVI. THE ANNUNCIATION. Painted after
Arezzo frescoes. Perugia, Art Gallery. Upper part
of altar, formerly in Sant' Antonio delle Monache,
Perugia. See next plate. (Photo: Anderson.)

XXXVII. MADONNA AND CHILD WITH STS ANTHONY,
JOHN THE BAPTIST, FRANCIS AND ELIZABETH. Lower
part of the altar of which the upper part is reproduced in
the last plate. (Photo: Anderson.)

XXXVIII. (*Opposite*) MADONNA AND CHILD. Detail from
Plate XXXVII.

XXXIX. BATTISTA SFORZA, DUCHESS OF URBINO. C. 1465.
Tempera on wood. 47×33 cm. Florence, Uffizi. Forms a diptych with
opposite plate. (Photo: Anderson.)

XL. FEDERIGO DI MONTEFELTRO, DUKE OF URBINO. Forms a diptych with opposite plate. See next two plates, and compare Plate XLVIII. (Photo: Anderson.)

XLI. TRIUMPH OF FEDERIGO MONTEFELTRO. Reverse of last plate.
(Photo: Anderson.)

XLII. TRIUMPH OF BATTISTA SFORZA. Reverse of Plate XXXIX. (Photo: Anderson.)

XLIII. (*Opposite*) MADONNA WITH TWO ANGELS. (Called the *Madonna di Sinigallia.*)
Late work. Tempera (?) on wood. 61×53·5 cm. Urbino, Art Gallery.
(Photo: Anderson.)

XLIV. THE NATIVITY. Late work. Tempera on wood. 126×123 cm. London, National
Gallery. View of Borgo San Sepolcro in background.

XLV. ST MICHAEL AND THE
DRAGON. Tempera on wood,
133 × 58 cm. London, National
Gallery. The authenticity of this
work has been questioned. It is
the left wing of an altarpiece of
which the right, representing St
Nicholas of Tolentino, is in the
Poldi-Pezzoli Gallery at Milan.

XLVI. (*Opposite*) MADONNA AND
CHILD WITH SAINTS, FOUR
ANGELS AND FEDERIGO DI MONTE-
FELTRO. c. 1475. Milan, Brera.
(Photo: Alinari.)

XLVII. STS JOHN THE BAPTIST, BERNADINE AND JEROME. Detail from Plate XLVI.

XLVIII. (*Opposite*) FEDERIGO DI MONTEFELTRO. Detail from Plate XLVI. Compare Plate XL.